New Goose

Lorine Niedecker

NEW GOOSE

edited by
Jenny Penberthy

❖

RUMOR BOOKS
Listening Chamber
Berkeley

❖

ISBN: 0-9639321-6-0

Acknowledgment: a selection of 29 of these poems were previously
printed in *West Coast Line* No. 7 (1992), editor, Roy Miki, in a Lorine
Niedecker Feature section, along with an introductory note, photos, and
an essay, "'The Revolutionary Word': Lorine Niedecker's Early Writings
1928-1946," both note and essay by Jenny Penberthy.

Cover art: Amy Trachtenberg
Typesetting & design: Steve Dickison
Back cover photo of Lorine Niedecker, 1929.
(Courtesy of the Dwight Foster Public Library, Fort Atkinson, Wisconsin)

New Goose is published as RUMOR BOOKS No. 1 in 2002 by
LISTENING CHAMBER
1605 Berkeley Way
Berkeley CA 94703

All orders: SPD/Small Press Distribution, Inc., www.spdbooks.org

CONTENTS

Editor's Note

THIS BOOK COLLECTS THE 86 POEMS that survive from Lorine Neidecker's Mother Goose-influenced period—1935 to 1945. Their first appearance was a 17-poem selection titled "Mother Geese" published in *New Directions* 1 (1936). By 1939, Niedecker had renamed the project *New Goose* suggesting both self-mockery and a contemporary response to a traditional form. The *New Goose* poems share the anti-authoritarian, subversive bent of their models, reflecting on the politics and economics of the time—the Depression, free market economics, socialism, and war.

Also within the orbit of the project are Wisconsin history and speech habits, Niedecker's immediate family, and her experience as a writer and reader.

Many of the poems have the tight rhythmic and rhyming symmetries of their Mother Goose forbears although the predictability of the form often clashes with the unresolved riddling and cryptic content. Other poems attend closely to the rhythms of idiosyncratic speech.

"Poetry is the folktales of the mind," she wrote to her Fort Atkinson friend Mary Hoard. Certainly the forms of these poems tap into childhood and communal memory, into the intuitive faculty and the unconscious. Throughout her career she was drawn to what she called the "heat given off by the mind." The nonsensical, the zany, the aleatoric, familiar to her from her early Surrealist writing, held continuing appeal.

"I am close to Tristan Tzara" she told Ezra Pound in 1934. In the spirit of proximity to Tzara, the nursery rhyme, and Niedecker's own anti-hierarchic practice, I have organized this collection as an alphabet book.

Some of these poems were revised for post-1945 contexts. Their history of variants and successive appearances is recorded in the notes to *Lorine Niedecker: Collected Works* published by the University of California Press. Thanks, as always, to Cid Corman for permission to publish.

—Jenny Penberthy

JENNY PENBERTHY is editor of *Lorine Niedecker: Collected Works,* published by the University of California Press; *Lorine Niedecker: Woman & Poet*, National Poetry Foundation; and *Niedecker and the Correspondence with Zukofsky 1931-1970,* Cambridge. She lives in Vancouver, British Columbia.

New Goose

A country's economics sick
affects its people's speech.

No bread and cheese and strawberries
I have no pay, they say.

Till in revolution rises
the strength to change

the undigestible phrase.

❖

A lawnmower's one of the babies I'd have
if they'd give me a job and I didn't get bombed
in the high grass

by the private woods. Getting so
when I look off my space I see waste
I'd like to mow.

❖

A monster owl
out on the fence
flew away. What
is it the sign
of? The sign of
an owl.

❖

A working man appeared in the street
in soldiers suit, no work, no peace.
What'r you doing in that dress,
a policeman said, where's the fight?
And after they took him for a ride
in the ambulance, they made arrest
for failure to molest.

❖

Allied Convoy
Reaches Russia

The ship that saved us—Uncle Joe!
Guns a quarter-mile long!

Red Comrades start their tanks in the hold,
climb in on the dock and are gone.

❖

Asa Gray wrote Increase Lapham:
pay particular attention
to my pets, the grasses.

❖

Ash woods, willow, close to shore,
gentle overflow each spring,
here he lived to be eighty-four
then left everything.

Heirs rush in—lay one tree bare
claiming a birdhouse, leave
wornout roof hanging there
nothing underneath.

If he could come back and see his place
fought over that he'd held apart
he'd say: all my life I saved
now twitter, my heart.

He owned these woods, every board,
till he lost his spring and fall;
if he could say: trees craved for—
overflow to all.

❖

Audubon

Tried selling my pictures. In jail
twice for debt. My companion
a sharp, frosty gale.

        In England unpacked
them with fear:
must I migrate back

to the woods unknown, strange
to all but the birds
I paint?

Dear Lucy, the servants here
move quiet
as killdeer.

❖

Not finding where the flowers were
he seized a tree.

. . .

Airplane or star?—so bright!
Star. I saw it last night.

❖

Birds' mating-fight
feathers floating down
offspring started
toward the ground.

❖

Black Hawk held: In reason
land cannot be sold,
only things to be carried away,
and I am old.

Young Lincoln's general moved,
pawpaw in bloom,
and to this day, Black Hawk,
reason has small room.

❖

You could go to the Underground's platform
for a three half-penny tube fare;
safe vaults of the Bank of England
you couldn't go there.

The sheltered slept
under eiderdown,
Lady Diana and the Lord himself
in apartments deep in the ground.

❖

Brought the enemy down
as his descendants, the bombs,
blew up Somerset House—

staircase at least—
where records go down
to Shakespeare who never ceased.

❖

O rock my baby on the tree tops
and blow me a little tin horn.
They've got us suckin the hind tit
and that's the way I was born.

O let me rise to the door-knob
and let me buy my way.
I know the owner of the store
and that's the way I was raised.

❖

Coopered at Fish Creek,
farmed at Egg Harbor,
teamed on the ice from Green Bay to Death's Door,
kept hotel till it burned,
fished and returned
to the Creek, then started for more.
Tennessee, Black Hills,
now my farm at Lost Lake,
and that'll be the end of J.E. Thorp.

❖

Don't shoot the rail!
Let your grandfather rest!
Tho he sees your wild eyes
he's falling asleep,
his long-billed pipe
on his red-brown vest.

❖

He kept a grog shop, this fur trader killer?
Defense: Any fur trader would
to make merchandise go. Moses Strong:
Inquire if the liquor was good.

He called Chief Oshkosh's daughter his wife?
Irrelevant!—John B. Du Bay
shot a man for claiming his land, enough
the possession of real estate.

Witnesses judged him as good as the average
for humanity, honesty, peace.
The court sent him home to his children,
his dogs, his gun, and his geese.

❖

For sun and moon and radio
farmers pay dearly;
their natural resource: turn
the world off early.

❖

From my bed I see
the wind willow
the grass.

From my head
in feathers comes
a gas.

I think of a tree
to make it
last.

❖

Gen. Rodimstev's story
(Stalingrad)

Four of us lived off half an acre
till grandfather traded it
for a gallon of liquor.

White Guards flogged father to death,
I studied to save
man's sweet breath.

❖

Grampa's got his old age pension,
$15 a month,
his own food and place.

But here he comes,
fiddle and spitbox . . .

Tho't I'd stop with you a little,
Harriut,
you kin have all I got.

❖

Hand Crocheted Rug

Gather all the old, rip and sew
the skirt I've saved so long,
Sally's valance, the twins' first calico
and the rest I worked to dye.
Red, green, black, hook,
hitch, nevermind, cramped
around back not yet the turn
of the century . . . Grandpa forward
from the shop, "Ought to have a machine."

❖

Here it gives the laws for fishing thru the ice—
only one hook to a line,
stay at the hole, can't go in to warm up,
well, we never go fishing, so they can't catch us.

❖

Hop press
                and conveyor for a hearse,
Newall Carpenter Senior's
                        two patented works.

                              . . .

Kilbourne. Eighteen sixty-eight.
Twelve hundred women and boys hopped.
When the market raced down to a dime a pound
from sixty-five cents, planters who'd staked
all they had, stopped.

❖

I doubt I'll get silk stockings out
of my asparagus
that grows too fast to stop it,
or any pair of Capital's
miracles of profit.

❖

I said to my head, Write something.
It looked me dead in the face.
Look around, dear head, you've never read
of the ground that takes you away.
Speed up, speed up, the frosted windshield's
a fern spray.

❖

I spent my money
by the ocean
and have not any
to fill a tooth.

❖

I walked
from Chicago to Big Bull Falls (Wausau),
eighteen-forty-four,
two weeks,
little to eat.
Came night
I wrapped myself in a piece of bark
and slept beside a log.

❖

I'm a sharecropper
down here in the south.
Housing conditions are grave.

We've a few long houses
but most folks, like me,
make a home out of barrel and stave.

❖

In the picture soldiers
moving thru a field
of flowers,
Spanish reds,
the flowers of war
move cautiously
not to tread
the wild heads.

Here we last,
lilacs, vacant lots,
taxes, no work,
debts, the wind widens
the grass,
in the old house
the clocks are dead,
past dead.

❖

Jim Poor's his name
and Poor Jay's mine,
his hair's aflame
not worth a dime

          or he'd sell it.

❖

Just before she died
my little grandma with her long, long hair
put her hand on mine: I'm nearly there.

What'll I do all my life,
I cried, my work's cut short; I've a share
in the speed-up; a long, long race to spare.

❖

Lady in the Leopard Coat

Tender spotted
hoped with care
she's coming back
from going there.

❖

Look, the woods, the sky, our home.

It's going to rain and if we're wise
we'll go in the wood and get us home
some chunks to keep us warm.

And while we're cutting trees it rains
and we are wise to go home
to keep from getting stiff and great.

❖

Missus Dorra
came to town
to buy some silkalene.
The clerk said Oh
my dear Mrs. Morra
is it in style ageen?

All these years
I saved and saved
and saved my silkalene
and yesterday
I threw it away—
how would taffeta be?

No, taffeta
cracks from hanging, besides
it's not being worn.
Mrs. Porra my dear
if you're going to be hung
won't crêpe do as weel?

❖

Motor cars
        like china
sometimes chink each other.

Will the speeding sugar bowl
        of taffy color
stop to eat people?

❖

Mr. Van Ess bought 14 washcloths?
Fourteen washrags, Ed Van Ess?
Must be going to give em
to the church, I guess.

He drinks, you know. The day we moved
he came into the kitchen stewed,
mixed things up for my sister Grace—
put the spices in the wrong place.

❖

My coat threadbare
over and down Capital Hill
fashions mornings after.

In this Eternal Category's
land of rigmarole
see thru the laughter.

❖

My daughters left home
I was certified,
then for weeks I raked leaves
                in New Madrid.

Now they tell me my girls
should support me again
and they're not out of debt
                from the last time they did.

❖

My man says the wind blows from the south,
  we go out fishing, he has no luck,
   I catch a dozen, that burns him up,
I face the east and the wind's in my mouth,
but my man has to have it in the south.

❖

No retiring summer stroke
nor the dangerous parasol
on the following sands,
no earth under fire flood lava forecast,
not the pop play of tax, borrow or inflate
but the radiant, tight energy
boring from within
communizing fear
into strike,
work.

❖

Not feeling well, my wood uncut.
                    And why?
The street's bare-legged young girls
    in my eye

with their bottoms out (at home they wear
                    long robes).
        My galoshes
    chopped the cold

till cards in The Moon where I sawed my mouth
                    to make the bid.
And now my stove's too empty
    to be wife and kid.

    ❖

Nothing nourishing,
common dealtout food;
no better reading
than keeps us destitute.

❖

O let's glee glow as we go
there must be things in the world—
Jesus pay for the working soul,
fearful lives by what right hopeful
and the apse in the tiger's horn,
costume for skiing I have heard
and rings for church people
and glee glo glum
it must be fun
to have boots for snow.

❖

Old Hamilton hailed the man from the grocery store:
What's today, Friday? Thursday! Oh,
nothing till tomorrow.

❖

On Columbus Day he set out for the north
to inspect his forty acres,
brought back a plaster of Paris deer-head
and food from the grocers and bakers,

a wall-thermometer to tell if he's cold,
a new kind of paring knife,
and painted in red, a bluebottle gentian
for the queen, his wife.

❖

Petrou his name was sorrow
and little did he know
they called him Tomorrow
and Today let him go.

❖

Pioneers

Anson Dart pierced the forest,

                    fell upon wild strawberries.
Frosts, fires, land speculation, comet.

                      Corn to be planted.
How to keep the strawberries?—

                    Indians' sugar full of dirt.
How to keep the earth.

Winnebagoes knew nothing
of government purchase of their land,
agency men got chiefs drunk
then let them stand.

On the steamer *Consolation*

                  came Dart's wife and daughters,
already there his sons and three sides of the house.
In the Great Bitter Winter a rug closed the side

                    that was bare.
For mortar they bored out a white-oak log,
pounded enough corn for a breakfast Johnnie cake
by rising—all sons—at 4:00.
Could be more, could be warmer, could be more.
Sun, turn the earth once more.

. . .

Between fighting fourteen nations' invading troops
and starting the first thousand-acre farms
    we hungered,
an effort to rise or stand up straight.

A tractor has seven hundred fifteen parts.
            I studied—
I'm a Morvin from the Eraya tribe—
                    learned all about oil and sand
the whole inner essence of the core.
Gorky recalls Professor Hvolson
                        lecturing on Einstein,
    clung with his hands to the pulpit,
swayed back and forth from lack of food.
Then—the first one!—red wheels
                    dipped, met the earth.
Red wheels gave the earth a new turn.

❖

Poet Percival said: I struck a load
but it was only a bunch in a chimney
without any opening
and as I left a sucker jumped me . . .
This is truly a rich and beautiful country.

❖

Remember my little granite pail?
The handle of it was blue.
Think what's got away in my life!
Was enough to carry me thru.

❖

See the girls in shorts on their bicycles
right here in Janesville. And why?—
no modesty anymore,
all gone by.

❖

Seven years a charming woman wore
her coat, removed the collar where it tore,
little warmth but honor in her loose
thin coat, without knowing why
she's so. Charming? Well, she's destitute.

❖

She had tumult of the brain
and I had rats in the rain
and she and I and the furlined man
were out for gain.

❖

She was a mourner too. Now she's gone
                    to the earth's core,
with organ notes, buried by church that buries the live,
intoning: That torture called by men delight
                    touches her no more.
So calm she looked, half smiling: Heaven?
                        No, restore
my matter, never free from motion,
            to the soil's roar.

❖

Summer's away, I traded my chicks for trees
so winter's tea-kettle on the high wood stove
       my feet to the heat
       my back in the shade
will tally with the tit-wit that sang
          from the upmost branch.

❖

Terrible things coming up,
these trailer houses.
People want to live in em,
park all over,
set out for somewhere,
never come home.

Nice!—
needn't clean anything,
just throw it out the window
onto somebody else.
Shiftless life!

❖

That woman!—eyeing houses.
She's moved in on my own poor guy.
    She held his hand and told him where to sign.

He gives up costs on his tree-covered shack—
insurance against wind, fire, falling aircraft, riots—
    home itself, was our break in the thick.

Because look! How can she keep it?—
to hold a house has to rent it out
    and spend her life on the street.

❖

The broad-leaved Arrow-head
grows vivid and strong
in my book, says: underneath
the surface of the stream the leaves
are narrow, long.
I don't investigate,
mark the page . . . I suppose
if I sat down beside a frost
and had no printed sign
I'd be lost. Well, up
from lying double in a book,
go long like a tree
and broad as the library.

❖

The brown muskrat, noiseless,
swims the white stream,
stretched out as if already
a woman's neck-piece.

In Red Russia the Russians
at a mile a minute
pitch back Nazi wildmen
wearing women.

❖

The clothesline post is set
yet no totem-carvings distinguish the Niedecker tribe
from the rest; every seventh day they wash:
worship sun; fear rain, their neighbors' eyes;
raise their hands from ground to sky,
and hang or fall by the whiteness of their all.

❖

The eleventh of progressional
the make-believe of prayer,
too many dunderoos
and everybody there.

If you stay at home
loving in the light
you'll always get an answer
wrong or right.

❖

The government men said Don't plant wheat,
we've got too much, just keep out weeds.

Our crop comes up thru change of season
to be stored for what good reason

way off and here we need it—Eat
who can, who can't—Don't grow wheat

or corn but quack-grass-bread!
Such things they plant around my head.

❖

The land of four o'clocks is here
the five of us together
            looking for our supper.
Half past endive, quarter to beets,
seven milks, ten cents cheese,
            lost, our land, forever.

❖

The Marshal of France made a speech,
told the people they were hungry.
The psychologist said: reach a porterhouse steak—
place your ounce of beef on a doll's plate.
The Bishop beseeched the people to sleep.

❖

The museum man!
I wish he'd taken Pa's spitbox!
I'm going to take that spitbox out
and bury it in the ground
and put a stone on top.
Because without that stone on top
it would come back.

❖

The music, lady,
you demand—
the brass
breaks my hand.

❖

The number of Britons killed
by German bombs equals
the number of lakes in Wisconsin.

But more German corpses
in Stalingrad's ruins
than its stones.

❖

Their apples fall down
and rot on the ground—
they don't spray their trees,
trees need care.
You can tell they're no good
that live there.

Apples are high—
that shows they're scarce,
still the stores always seem to have plenty.
Can't get a price
the farmers say—
I guess it's because there'r too many.

❖

There was a bridge once that said I'm going
and a cistern that said What Ho
and the stick said lying on the ground
how am I to grow?

❖

There's a better shine
on the pendulum
than is on my hair
and many times

. .   . .

I've seen it there.

❖

They came at a pace
to go to war.

They came to more:
a leg brought back
to a face.

❖

To a Maryland editor, 1943:
The enclosed poems are sepa-
rated by stars to save paper.

Dear MacCloud:
the poems called Goose
separated by stars
to save the sun—

"We couldn't get away
with these down here
in the south of the brow
of Washington"—

appeared: your night's
folk-tongue.

❖

To see the man who took care of our stock
as we slept in the dark, the blackbirds flying
high as the market out of our pie,
I travel now at crash of day
on the el, a low rush of geese over those below,
to see the man who smiled
and gave us a first-hand country shake.

❖

To war they kept
            us going
but when the garden
            bloomed
I let them know
            my death.

With time war
            is splendid
and the rainbow
            sword,
they do not break
            my rest.

❖

Trees over the roof
and I was down
when the night
came in.

❖

Troubles to win
and battles to bin
and after
a tare in the side
of all my ties
                    and barn

                            dances.

❖

Van Gogh

At times I sit in the dunes,
faint, not enough to eat.
The path thru the dunes
is like a desert . . . the family's shoes
patched and worn and many more
such views.

❖

Voyageurs
sang, rowed
their canoes full of furs,

sang as they rowed.
Ten minutes every hour
rested their load.

❖

We know him—Law and Order League—
fishing from our dock,
testified against the pickets
at the plant—owns stock.

There he sits and fishes
stiff as if a stork
brought him, never sprang from work—
a sport.

❖

Well, spring overflows the land,
floods floor, pump, wash machine
of the woman moored to this low shore by deafness.

Good-bye to lilacs by the door
and all I planted for the eye.
If I could hear—too much talk in the world,
too much wind washing, washing
good black dirt away.

Her hair is high.
Big blind ears.

I've wasted my whole life in water.
My man's got nothing but leaky boats.
My daughter, writer, sits and floats.

❖

What a woman!—hooks men like rugs,
clips as she hooks, prefers old wool, but all
childlike, lost, houseowning or pensioned men
her prey. She covets the gold in her husband's teeth.
She'd sell dirt, she'd sell your eyes fried in deep grief.

❖

When do we live again Ann,
when dirt flies high
in wheeling time
and the lights of their eyes see ours.
For if it's true
we're the dung of the earth
and they the flowers
from stock that's running out
they need to be planted over.

They'll never know
the weeping diff'rence, Ann,
when the whole world laughs again.

❖

When Johnny (Chapman) Appleseed
came to a place he didn't like
he covered it with apple trees.
He was the early American apple
who changed the earth by dropping seeds.

He walked all over the mid-west states.
His trees grew while he slept.
Gave to the poor tho he himself
lived on roots and had no bed.

Nor had he a wife. Nor creed
that embraced grafting. Johnny
reproduced by seed.

❖

Woman with Umbrella

Lonely woman, not prompted
by freshness from the sky
to run with friends and laugh it off,
arrives unsparkling but dry—

she's felt the prongs of her own advance
thru the crowded street,
knows that lonely
she is dangerous to meet.

❖

Young girl to marry,
winds the washing harry.

❖

*Printed in an edition
of 3000 copies
Summer 2002*

❖

RUMOR BOOKS

"She too is somehow a goddess"

—Hesiod, *Works & Days*
tr. M.L. West

Beginning with the publication in 2002
of American poet Lorine Niedecker's classic early work
written over the course of the Great Depression and World
War II, *Rumor Books* proposes to bring into print in
handsome small editions a number of similarly fugitive,
hard-to-come-by, or yet-to-appear works from the century
just passed: books *rumored to exist*. In preparation,
scheduled for publication during 2003, is translator
Chris Daniels' edition of selected poems by 20th-century
Brazilian master Modernist poet Murilo Mendes—
Chaos's Window. Later books to be announced.

❖

No. 1
Lorine Niedecker, *New Goose*
edited by
Jenny Penberthy

No. 2
Murilo Mendes, *Chaos's Window*
translated by
Chris Daniels

Published by
LISTENING CHAMBER
Berkeley

Editor
Steve Dickison

Distributed by
SPD/Small Press Distribution, Inc.
1341 Seventh Street
Berkeley CA 94710

All orders foreign *&* domestic
800-869-7553
www.spdbooks.org

❖